DAR: A Super Girly Top Secret (

Volume One

by Erika Moen

www.darcomic.com

DAR has been my online journal comic since 2003.
This volume, however, only collects strips from mid 2006-08 since that's when it started sucking less.
Erika of 2009

WAIT, WAIT! You can't throw new readers into the middle of your comic with no context!
Hm, well then I guess we'll just have to have a...

THREE YEAR RECAP

2003
I loooove you!
I loooooove you too!
First girlfriend

NOOOOOOO
She left me for her ex!
SOB SOB
ANGST
ANGST
ANGST
Love is a lie!

First Tattoo

Introduction

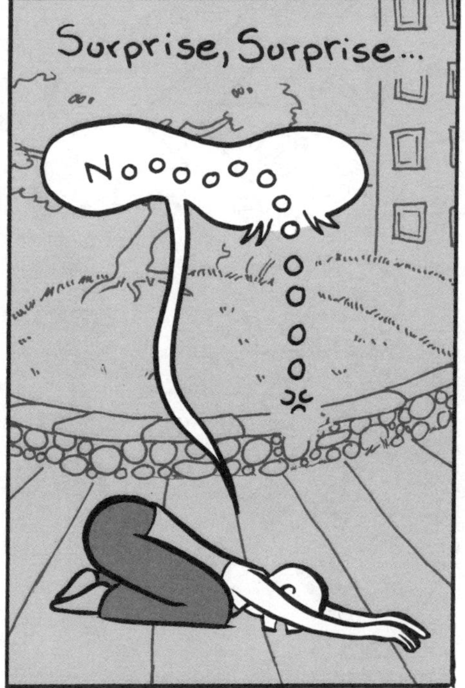

Anyone who lives abroad and isn't changed by it is doing something wrong.
second tattoo

Aix-en-Provence provided boundless beauty and inspiration.

...and get...

One weekend I went to London.
Oh god, I'm staying with a fan of my comics I've hardly emailed in a country I've never visited?
What's WRONG with me??
Erika?

ZING
I'm Matt!
HOMINA

Who knows when I'll ever be attracted to another man? I HAVE to act on this.
American lesbians sure are friendly...

Quarterly-hourly texts, daily calls, a couple weekend visits and a month-long backpacking expedition across France later...
I... I love him.

But I'm GAY.
AND I still love my ex!
Oh God, WHO AM I??
HE'S BROKEN MY IDENTITY.

Lissen' here boy-O, this is JUST my fling abroad.
When I go home, life returns to NORMAL.
Cool, cool.
I'm just glad we got to spend this time together.

Now boarding flight 335 to the United States.
I love you.
I love you too.

I've really missed you...
My ex wants to see me!
But she treats me like shit...
And I... miss Matt?

Hey Matt,
You make me happy. Let's make this work.

2006

Odd things that made me orgasm

and ONE and TWO and ONE and TWO... double time!
working out.

Kissing.

Giving someone else a blowjob.
mmmm—? hey?

vibrations from an escalator.

vibrations from a bus.
vrrrrm!

Having here licked.

rustle
rustle
The sound of a bean bag chair.

Breast play

Almost
from being spanked.

Watching a White Stripes video.

Having my belly button licked.

They're all true!
I can't help it!

Gloup

Getting with a lesbian really isn't as great as straight guys would hope.

BunnyLuv

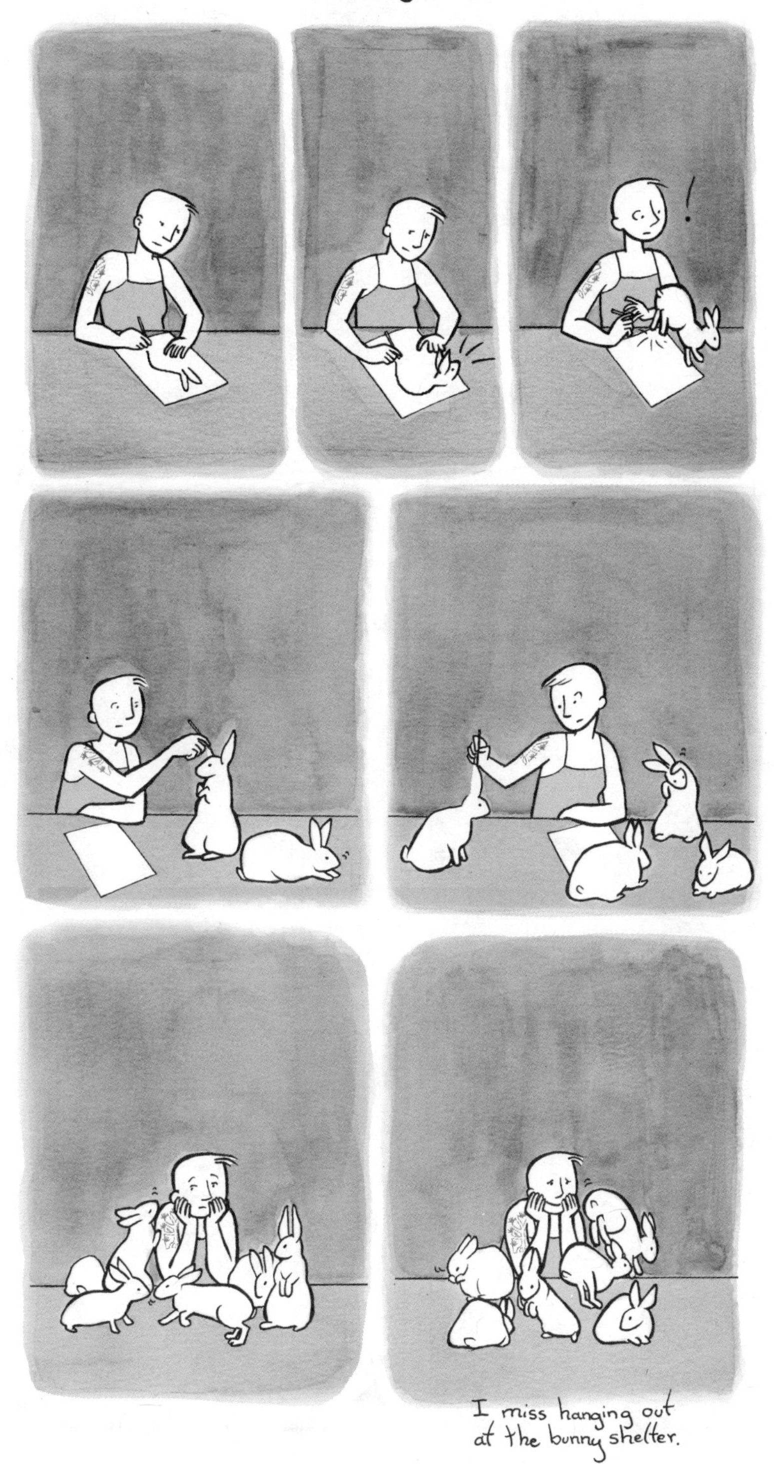
!
I miss hanging out
at the bunny shelter.

I Like a Boy

I love women.
Naturally I'm comfortable around them...
...and jesus am I attracted to them.
It's pretty safe to say that I'm in
LESBO TERRITORY

But then I met Matt.
?

Erika?
...you okay?
orgasm coma
Does this make me a bisexual?

boys who aren't Matt
BLEH.

As much as Matt rocks my world and I enjoy being physical with him, theres a nagging sense of
I... I've fallen for a lamp!
Dude, that ain't right.

I Like a Boy

Even when I'm with girls I have nothing in common with I am still enchanted with their bodies
I want to feel every curve and just melt into them.
Boys...
...boys are different.

I like him.

The minute we met, I knew on a gut level that this was a person I wanted in my life.

I like a boy.

Attack!

Typa tap tap tip typitty type tap tap tap type
PEEK!
deek-i- deek-i- deek-i-
Oh my god, Lindsay. This is the worst paper I've ever written.
I like to pinch.
WAHG!
Poing!

Attack!

No!!
Lindsay!
ow!
ow!
Stop!!
yeek!
AHK!
ow
ow!
deek-i-deek-i-deek-i-...
AHHHHHHGG!!
April 20, 2006

Phllrp

Watching a movie
Phhhxxxxpptttt...
rustle
Snf
Snf
SNOFF?
Oh... Oh GOD, Erika!
L... Love me?
No!
LOVE ME!
It's rancid!
You've gone off lady!
I just want you to love me!
Seriously, see a doctor for your insides!
Admit that you like it!
God, I can't even breath!
Come baaaack!
Never.
I wana cuddle.
We're divorced
Fine, I hate you
Good, I hate you too.
Great, then we're even.
Guess we are.
5 minutes later.
Phlrp!
shift

Erika's last 7 months:
The Condensed Version.

January:
Flew to France for my semester abroad...
Aix-en-Provence, France
California, USA

...where I lived with Raymonde.
She's the most awesome left-wing grandma political activist **ever**!
Cou-Cou!

Kind of learned French (but not really)
'Cos all my attention was devoted to drawing and comics — I was **hella** productive over here.

(also I was angsting over my break up with Marni.)
She loves me, I know she does– so why won't she commit?? WHY DOESN'T SHE WANT TO **MARRY** ME???

A reader I'd never talked with before hooked me up with a place to stay for London's comic expo thing.
Hi, I'm Matt!
English accent
Dude... he's cute. (???)

Maintained contact with Marni.
gab
gab
gab
I love you
I love you
I love you

The Last Seven Months

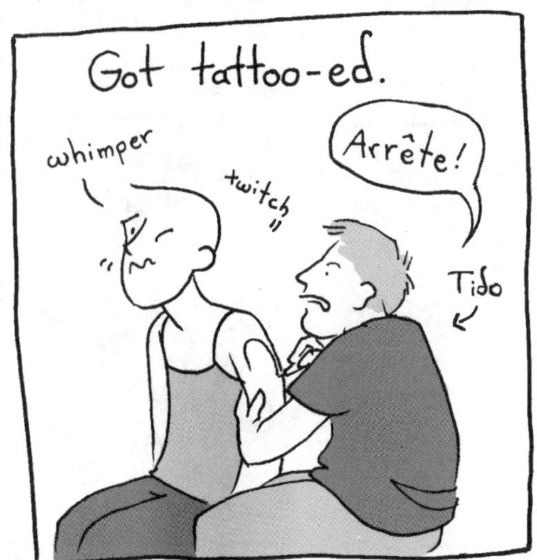

The Last Seven Months

Finished school, travelled France for a month with Matt.
Onward!
Designated joint-roller

Returned to the States.
ZOOM!

Stayed with my family for a week.
rrrr

Moved to Portland for the summer.
I live with them
Kip
Bill
Jenn
Dylan

Ended things with Marni.
SOB
Pat Pat

Which brings us to July where I can't find a job and am pretty much living off profits from my comics and art sales.
Matt
C'mon, c'mooo°n! Bid more! I wanna buy groceries!
Ping!

DONE

Daily Grind

6:00
GUH!
DEET DEET DEET DEET DEET DEET DEET
WAKE UP
6:15
G'mornin' Matt!
er, afternoon for you, I guess...
BREAKFAST
7:15
GETTING to CARPOOL
7:30
What th'shit am I doing?
...oh God... WHAT THE SHIT AM I DOING?
CARPOOLING to WORK
8:00- 1:00
secs frames shot run time
$00.0 → 03.14 sec
makes 3 secs x 24 frames = 72 + 14 secs = 86 frames
Oh God, is this all I'm good for?
click click click click click
EARNING $$$
1:05
Hey Matt!
Miss you lots.
Works okay...
LUNCH
2:00- 7:00
I'm not good enough to be an artist.
This is what I'll be doing for the rest of my life.
DATA ENTRY
DATA ENTRY
DATA ENTRY
EARNING $$$
7:30
What am I doing?
What am I doing?
What am I doing with my life?
GOING HOME
8:00
...so... tired...
fwump!
THE END?

Things I Do When I'm Stressed

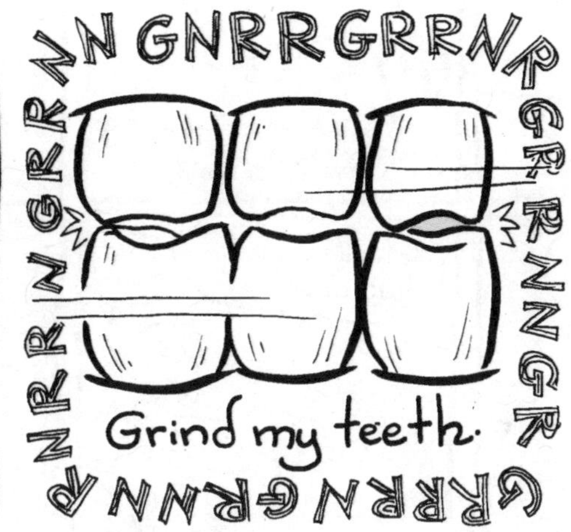

The Little Things

The Little Things

Withdrawl

a-type-typa-type-tap-
-tap-tip-
XWEEK
thump
...type...tap-tap-type-
-type-type-tap-
-type-type-type-tappity
-tap-tap-tip-
...type...type...tap-tap-

Withdrawl

Withdrawl

Going to see Stormy dance @
DEVIL'S POINT
I'm scared!
It'll be fuuuuun
Spotting Suicide Girls
It's London!
STRIPPERS!
KICK
Booo
I'm in love!
sketchy guy
Strip Club Etiquette?
Are we sitting at the stage too long?
Everyone else pops in and out!
Do we look like creepniks?
Shaddup.
Stripper Misshaps!
It's stuuuuuck!
Hold still!
Corset caught on fishnets.
finally...
Stormy!
Hey, she is cute!
duuur.
SHOVE
Best lapdance EVER
my shirt
on stage!
slurp slurp
Actually said this
My favorite lollipop!
(She got more tips during my dance than any of her other performances.)
And the highlight...
meeeerWAH!
Man, watta night!
Maaatt, I'm tired!
Also outta $$$
nickle
But it's only 2am!

2007

Tea Kisses

Tea bags

Hot water
?

Something sweet
Sugar
Honey

Let cool
Slp-
OW
really!

Drink
Sllllp!

Tea kisses!
smp

Coffee Crush

I know she does it for everyone...
..but I still have such a crush.

Portland Rain

This is absolutely true:

SQUISH
I love playing with my boobs

Bo
$
Jangrs
STATS
Cute, perkier, favored among lovers
STATS
Larger, hangs, scarred from tumor removal.

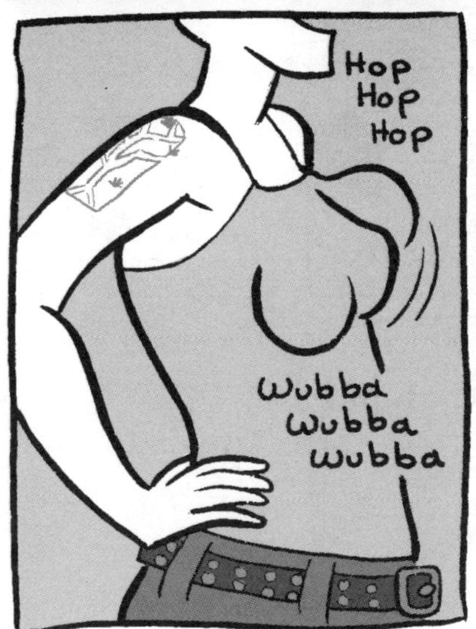
Hop
Hop
Hop
Wubba
Wubba
Wubba

Sometimes they have ridiculous growth spurts.
wad'ja do?
It just happened five minutes ago!
But they always go back to normal.

I love you guys.
We love you too!

And we all live happily ever after.

Youthful Expectations

for the Queen

QUESTION:
is it hard to write about people you know?
What're you up to today?
Drawing a whole new DAR 'cos the one I was doing got too personal.
Really! How?
It was about my new pelvis problems n' after I was half way through I was like, 'The internet really doesn't need to know about my gunky vagina.'
Haha, yeah
What are you replacing it with.
The strip where you claim my butt. In the name of England? From when I visited in December.
I what?
You grabbed my ass and were all 'I claim this butt in the name of England!'
Oh. Hm.
What?
You always make me out as a big British stereotype.
Wh-what?
No, honey!
It's a cute story, that's all!
Yeah, well, you always play up that I'm British—
And I'm not even!
... You live there and have the accent...
It just feels like every comic I'm in is about my cultural difference.
The last one was just us talking!
It was you talking at me - I had one line and no personality.
I'm... I'm sorry, I didn't know you felt like that.
Do you not want me to use this comic?
No, no.
'Cos I won't if you don't want me to!

No, you already scrapped your other strip.
Maybe just include a note saying I'm not the British stereotype you show.
Geez, Matt, I'm sorry...
It's okay!
I'm not upset, it's just...
It's just very one-sided.
flashback!
2002
Liz
Wow, I really sound like a bitch.
coffee to Go
2004
Marni
You make me out as a heartless dick.
Various she-dumped-me comics
2007
Matt
Your readers think I'm a British stereotype.
DAR
Beep
ANSWER:
only if you have a conscience.

Pizza and Coke for dinner.
muncha munch
glub glb
BRURP!
ffcthp!
HrrUrrpp!
nice.

Zit face

*Specifically refers to pulling out hair, but the characteristics are identical.

Electricity

I'm going to CONQUER the fuckin' WORLD
After graduating I was electrified.

I got a vibrant tattoo
symbolizing my boundless energy.

Then I moved to Portland, got a nice, steady job,
and settled into a comfortable routine.

Not even a year had passed
and my tattoo was dramatically fading.

I know where I want to be as a Grown Up
MFA
Professional cartoonist
Honey! I'm home!
spouse
Published Work
Success!

SOCIAL LIFE
INSUR
OPPORTUNITY
FREELA
SECURITY
SAVINGS
LOVE
but I don't know how to get there.

I'm scared I won't have what it takes.
opportunity
opportunity
Oh, I couldn't catch those anyway.

Can't fail if I don't try!
oppor
opp
... but isn't that failing too?

Where did my electricity go?

Bike Accident

If you've visited Portland,
you know this sign.

That's because our streets are populated by VISCIOUS rails,
Mwa-ha-HAH!
HUNGRY for innocent, succulent bike wheels.

You... you get where this is going, right?
AHG!

You okay?
...urrrg...
The cement was very warm.

The Damage
Handlebars and wheel mis-aligned
Scrape
Bruise
Bruise
Could have been worse!

...Hey Indy, can you give me a ride?
Me: 0
Portland: 1

Toast

I am my own toaster

Clogged

10/4/07

Helping Hands

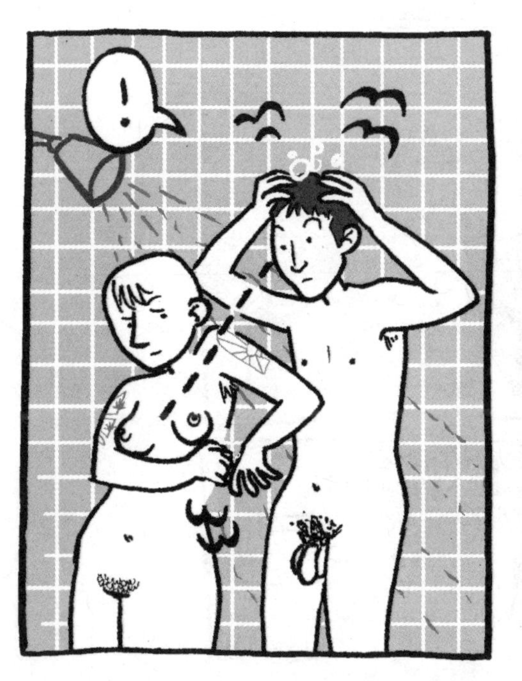

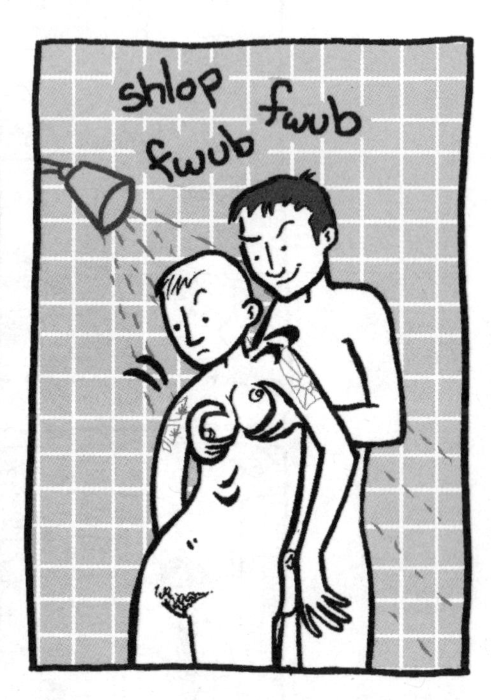

Stumptown Comics Fest 2007

September has been
COMICS MADNESS
copies!
draw draw
k-chung!
click click
preparing for the 4th annual Stumptown Comics Fest.

Stumptown is Portland's comics and arts convention that caters towards artists.

Sarah Oleksyk and I were speakers at the Zinesters Talking lecture series for the library.
ROADSIDE

My best friend, Leslie Levings, came up from Los Angeles!
Her Beastlies!!

... Now fold the strip over every edge...
Like this?
I get people to stop at my table by teaching how to make origami stars.

I moderated Special Guest Sarah Oleksyk's spotlight panel
Tell us about your latest project.
Well...
(Unrelated to our earlier talk!)

Hey!
You've gotta pay for that!
Curses!
Matt stopped a douche from nicking Leslie's Beastlies while she was in the bathroom.

Shannon "Too Much Coffee Man" Wheeler and I tied for Stumptown's Outstanding DIY award!

It was good,
I'm inspired,
I feel validated...
but I'm glad it's over.

The Best Job

At the Stumptown Comics Fest...
slllp
!
You did the Devil's Point comic?
Uh, yeah...
I'm a dancer there! We love this comic!
No way!
Yeah, we have it up in the dressing room!
No WAY!
Stormy loves it.
Oh jeez, I have such a crush on Stormy.
Haha, who doesn't?
The next time I see her, I'll tell her I met you.
Cool, thanks!
That night...
From: Rocket
To : Erika
RE: from Rocket and Stormy
Hello! Rocket here. It was good to see you at Comic Fest.
gasp!
"I worked at Devil's Point later with stormypants and took some pics for you with my trusty camera.
I ♡ erika
I ♡ erika
Enjoy!"
And that's when I truly understood how being a cartoonist is the most rewarding job in the WORLD.
more strippers

Thanks again to Stormy and Rocket, Portland's hottest strippers!

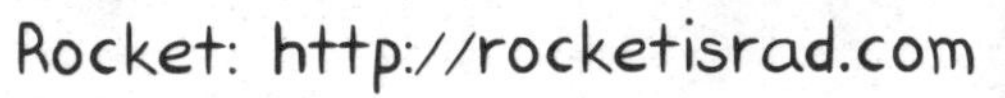

Stormy: www.myspace.com/stormy_is_dope

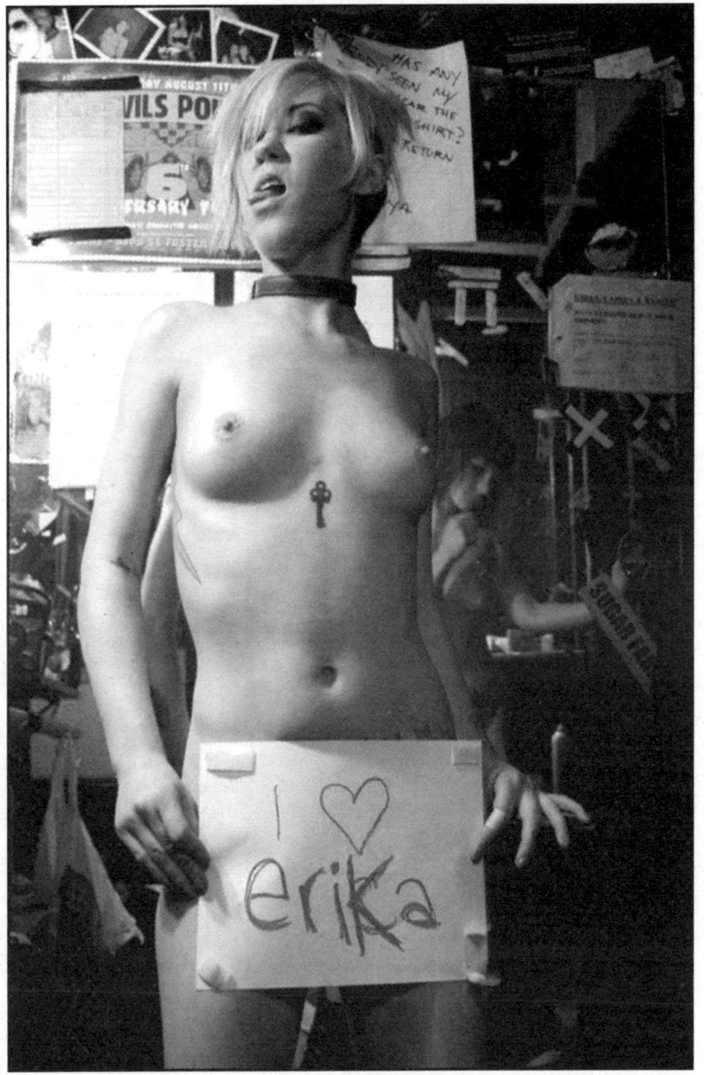

Oh Dear

Holy shit, DEER!!
muncha munch
Matt's mom took us to a deer park in England.

It's nibbling my fingers!
Nom Nom Nom

Knole Park is enormous.
Deer!

Fields of foxglove!
Bump!
Honey, hold your umbrella still.

Deer AND foxglove!!

It was a pretty rad day.
duuuur.
doink
Even tho' it turns out deer are pretty stupid lookin' close up.

By day I'm just another mediocre artist...
Sigh
... but by night I switch sides of the easel to become

Erika the
LIFE MODEL
extraordinaire
Hoo HAH!
Thas' RIGHT!

Dynamic!
negative space!
weird!
I pose the way I want to draw life models.

Surprisingly, it's very fulfilling!
People pay rapt attention to me,
My body feels strong and confident.
I'm being creative and it's being used in art!

It's so gratifying to actually **be good** at something I love to do!
draw
draw
draw
draw
erase
sketch

Honestly tho'...
Heh Heh!
TIPS
I just like the novelty of getting paid to be naked.

Spit Roast

Radio interview with "Flight of the Conchords"
"... And it was very awkward and embarrassing"
"It's unfortunate, but yeah, it was in England where they call a threesome a "**spit roast**" which is a very British term that we weren't familiar with..."

Ohmygod, the British call threesomes a "spit roast"??
... yeah...
It means a guy in the vag and a guy in the mouth.
!!!

... Baby... we've **talked** about it before.
I-
I thought we were talking about **dinner**.

Dyke with a Boyfriend

Cooking Accidents

Bring.
It.
ON.

I am terrified of cooking

Waittaminute, teaspoon not tablespoon!
That's because I'm awful at it.

"one clove of garlic"
...What's a clove?
Maybe that's how they say "a whole one"
TOSS!
My worst experience was the first time I tried to do it alone.
12/2/07

"Thinly slice the carr
Chop
chop
chop
chop
CHOP

Uh... Hey, Douglas?
C-Can you come over right now?
And bring your first aid kit?

Cooking: 1
Me : 0

EPILOGUE

(Turns out '**clove**' does **not** mean '**whole**')

The next night I made it again and it turned out pretty okay.

fashionista

Last night I had another intervention.
DON'T CUT YOUR HAIR.
You look so good now! If you just got it styled...
Over due for a buzz

I know that fashion and looking good are important in the professional world...
But I feel fake.

Buzz cuts and simple clothes just FEEL GOOD.
It's pure ME.

The older I get, the more I feel like a fashion outsider.
er...

It's only a matter of time before I ~~give up~~ er, grow up.
I could buy 14 comics for the same price.

I like your hair. I like how you dress.
rub rub
12/14/07
But I guess I can put it off a little longer

Segway Cops

I don't know if this is just a Portland thing...
My purse!
HAW!
I'm on it!
fan fan
zmmm
but our cops ride Segways.
the SEGWAY
·12.5 MPH
·105 Lbs
·Eco-friendly
·Lithium batteries
BAD ASS
Cop without a Segway:
Man, you smell bacon?
Yeah man, smells like PIG
Musn't... let them... see me cry!
Cop WITH a Segway:
SLAP!
SOB
Portland criminals?
FASTER!!
I pity you.
What can stop a cop on a Segway?
CRASH
NOTHING.
My hero!
Thank you, Segway cops!

2008

Today I'm introducing:
wubba wubba
my
COCK O' DOOM

Flashback!
It's finally here!
ORDERED:
$10 tiny butt plug

...uh...
RECEIVED:
$100 COCKOSAURUS

Obviously the company mixed up so I'm doing the right thing...
and giving it to you.
1/5/08

Tho' it's too big for its, uh, intended use,
Modeling for Dr. Sketchy's
it has not gone to waste.

One mystery remains:
what is the HEAVY DUTY chain for??

Housemate Conversation

INTRODUCING: my housemate, Matt Bernier!
He's a cartoonist too!
(Not to be confused with my boyfriend, Matt Nolan.)

G'morning!
Hey, you don't usually wear glasses.

Yeah, I dunno, I prefer contacts, definitely.
Well, you look better with glasses.

What, really?
Yeah, they compliment your head shape.
1/13/08

My... head shape? Does it look bad without glasses?
Oh, jeez!
That's like one of those awful "Does this dress make me look fat??" questions.

ARE YOU CALLING ME FAT?!

Financial Stability

Butt Sex

Ow.
Ow.
Ow.
Ow.
Ow.
Ow.
Ow.
Ow.
pat
pat
pat

Ow.
Ow. Ow.
Ow.

Ow.
How ya doin'?
Ow.

I got too excited and pushed back harder than I meant to.

I Know.
Ow.
This happens every time.
Ow.
1/27/08

BUTT SEX:
Go slow.
Ow.
This message brought to you by my ass hole.

Love Lost

Sooooooo GOOD
nearing orgasm
PNU
I used to eat peanut butter every day.

something's ... wrong...
PNU
...until my 23rd year.

SWELL

Sounds like you're allergic.
But I don't have any allergies!
Also, I love peanuts in a near sexual way.

I had to get to the bottom of this in the scientific way:
with a GIANT BOWL of PEANUTS.
2/2/08

Oooooh jesus....
I am hella allergic.

Sweet Talk

Kiss

You're my honey.
Because you taste sweet.
Awww!

You're my girlfriend because...
you're...
a girl?

The Origins of DAR

This week I'm answering QUESTIONS from th' READERS

"Dear Erika,
What the hell does DAR mean?
Love,
Every Reader, Ever."
I'm so glad you asked!

Back in my college days, instead of saying DUH, I said
DAR!

2003
Shit! What do I call this fucker?
completed comics
unfinished homework
My whole life I have been cursed with title-writing block.

Well, it's an auto-bio strip about my stupid life...
...Which is the most self-indulgent kind of comic there is...

I'll just give it an equally stupid, self-indulgent title!
"DAR: A Super Girly Top Secret Comic Diary"
Haha, PERFECT.
Shit, not like it's gunna go anywhere, any-way...
2/17/08

2008
Seriously, what the fuck does DAR mean?
I hate you, Erika of 2003.

Car Accident

On Saturday, I made cupcakes with my new friends, Rachel and Randy.
cupcake-wich
Red velvet with cream cheese frosting!

They were driving me home on the I-205 when...
Bla Blah Bl-
ZOOM ZOOM ZOOM SKREET
!!! fuck! fuck! fuck!
skreeeeee
Ohmygod, that was clo-
ZOOM ZOOM

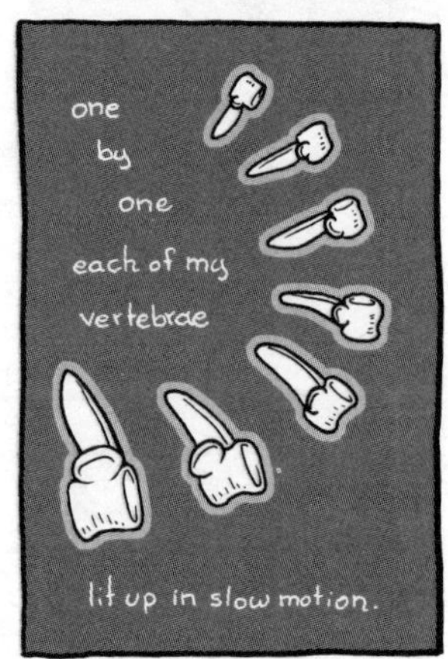
one
by
one
each of my
vertebrae
lit up in slow motion.

Though the rear-ender was at fault, when the cop found out Rachel is uninsured, we were the bad guys.

Because it is illegal to drive without insurance, we were all criminal suspects.
Turn around, hands behind your head, interlock your fingers.
Pat
Pat
Pat
Pat
Pat
Pat
The car got searched too.

Hey Kip? I, uh, have a favor to ask...
shiver shiver shiver
Rachel's car got towed and impounded.

My neck didn't warrant a brace, but the next day it did need some extra support.
Well, I feel classy!
ice pack tucked in back

Hey, you left the stove on again.
I have WHIPLASH! C'MON!!

If I Had A Penis

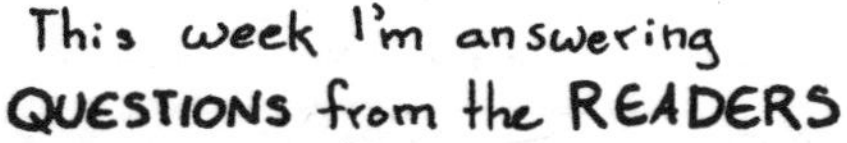
This week I'm answering
QUESTIONS from the READERS

"If you could have any super power, what would you choose?"
Hmmm
Honey, you would grow a dick.
Seriously, it's all you ever talk about.

Ohmygod, you're totally right!
You would be the worst person in the world to have a cock.
I KNOW.
You'd be arrested in five minutes.
But it'd be SO WORTH IT!

Hey! Hey, I'm waving hello!
Hi!
Hey!
Look at me!
sigh
waggle waggle

Oh God, it's even better than I could have hoped for...
plop
plop
plop
2/24/08

Look!
Look, I put your sunglasses on it!
It's a face now!
Baby?
Look!
SOB

Honey, there is a very real reason why God gave you a vagina.
...'n I could push elevator buttons...

Only Science Can Save Her Vagina

Downside to Long Distance

I can't wait to see you again, baby...
YOU'RE ON YOUR OWN FOR BACK ZITS.

Life Model Mishaps

Cat

Mrowr?
prowr?
I'm so glad humans perverted your species into snuggle-bots.
purr purr rrrrrr rrrrrr

Stumptown Comics fest 2008

Another year, another Stumptown Comics Fest
Why am I never ready?

Aw, really?
Don't spend it all in one place! - er, wait.
Indigo Kelleigh, Founder

I was touched to get a Thank You letter and gift certificate (to Cosmic Monkey Comics) for having attended **all 5 years** of the fest.

For the 4th year in a row, I was neighbors with **Team Atrox**
Frank
Paul
Jeff
Emory
Leslie

Meredith Gran was very patient while my shit kept spilling on her side of the table.
Sorry!
S'okay!

I got to moderate the Spot Light Panel for
Raina Telgemeier!
Hi!

My baby bro Erik even came down!
When did you get tall?
Uh...
Your voice changed??
I'm almost 21
I thought you were 16!!

I debuted the 2nd print volume of DAR...
DAR

...which won 3 awards!
OUTSTANDING DEBUT
OUTSTANDING WRITING
OUTSTANDING DIY
5/13/08

I love you, Stumptown!
See you next year!

Safe Word

It's not gay if the balls don't touch.

Truth in Autobiography

This week I'm answering **QUESTIONS** from the **READERS**

How true are your comics?
scribble scribble

What're you drawring?
Our fight from yesterday.

But you made it look like you won!
I did.

That's a bloody lie!
Nuh-uh!
I tickled you till you screamed banana!

You lost in two seconds and you know it.
...
5/26/08

Well you can just draw your own comics where you get to win.
True Enough.

The One About Queefing

Sex Accidents

The Worst Things I've Done to My Partners During Sex:

Dry humped a bald patch on his leg.

Blew in her Vag.

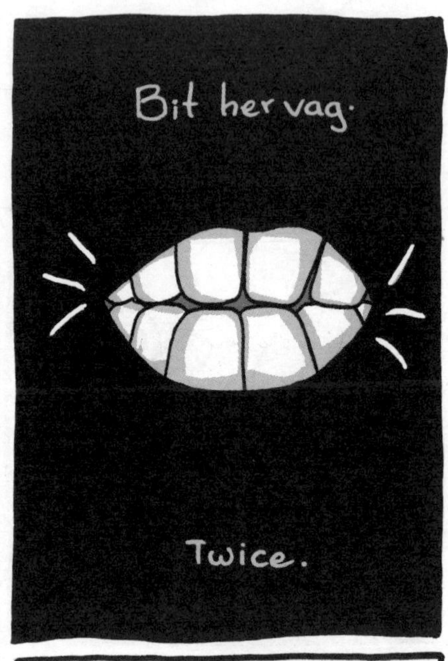
Bit her vag.
Twice.

frup
Oh GOD, It's IN MY MOUTH.
Farted while 69ing.

Ooh, I'd moan and run my hand up your ——
uh.
fuck.
I'll call you back later.
Wet farted during phone sex.

PHLORP
Queefed his day-old spunk back in his mouth.

I officially apologize for ever becoming sexually active.

A Little Exposition

Making friends

The Babysitter

Strawberry Picking

Some friends and I went STRAWBERRY PICKIN'!
U-P
One flat, please.
U-PICK
Cat
Susan
Anne

Oregon sure can be pretty.

Anne!
This one looks like it has genital warts!

TASTE COMPARISON
Grocery Store Strawberry
25%
tastiness
Wild Strawberry
110%
tastiness

Oh, the possibilities...

FREE ADVICE
Son of a...
Accidental jam
Be gentle when you rinse wild berries.

The Miracle fruit Party

Pranked

HAVE YOU EVER PULLED A PRANK ON SOMEONE?

BUT THEY NEVER NOTICE?

DYLAN MECONIS,

for the love of God, it's been, like, a week,

PLEASE CHECK YOUR FLICKR FAVORITES.

Shrinkage

Cold, cold shower!
Aw, I'm sorry, sweetie.

Now my cock'n balls are all tiny.
Really??

Bwah!

I love them!
You're supposed to be excited when they get bigger.

But when they're all tight and tiny in my hand, I feel like a benevolent giant protecting the villagers.

Don't worry Little Dudes, I'll keep you safe!

Phone Sex

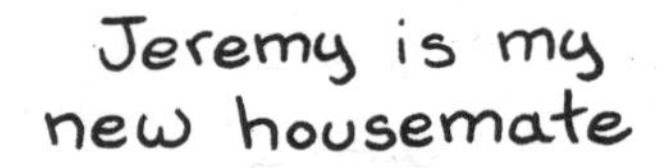

Jeremy is my new housemate

He used to be a phone sex operator

REALLY??
Well, only for like, a month.
They paid ¢.25 a minute and those calls don't really last that long, y'know?

When someone calls through an 800 number, they're verified to be over 18 so you can say whatever.

There is no cuddling in professional phone sex.

But if they call through a 900 number, they might be underage,
I touch your ...mounds?
List of substitution words
so you can't say anything explicitly sexual.

Wow, so you must be pretty good at phone sex now, huh?
Oh, I can't do it at all anymore.
It's kinda been ruined for me.

I tell you what, tho', guys **love** it when you tell them you stick your finger in their butt.
Hey honey, how y'doin'?
I stick my finger in your butt!

Strip Club Etiquette

DOUCHE BAGS!
at the strip club
All of the following I witnessed during one night at the Acropolis.

Eh?
Eh??
uh, no.
DON'T offer your tip in your mouth

smack
chew
chew
DON'T
eat at the rack

No matter how good the music is...
DON'T start dancing with your bros.

Seriously dudes, how is this NOT common sense??

Bike Slut

peddle
peddle
pump
pump
pump
peddle
peddle
peddle
puff
puff
pant
pant
bumpity
bumpity
bumpity
Hey Sweetie! Good ride?
Sex
NOW
Aww, did someone get horny on her bike?

gronkle SNORT
This is Josee

Don't start playing with her nipples,
shnurfle snuffle shnuff
because you won't be able to stop.
They feel like fat gummy worms.

All she wants is to love you
SHNURF
AHG!
by sharing her various fluids.

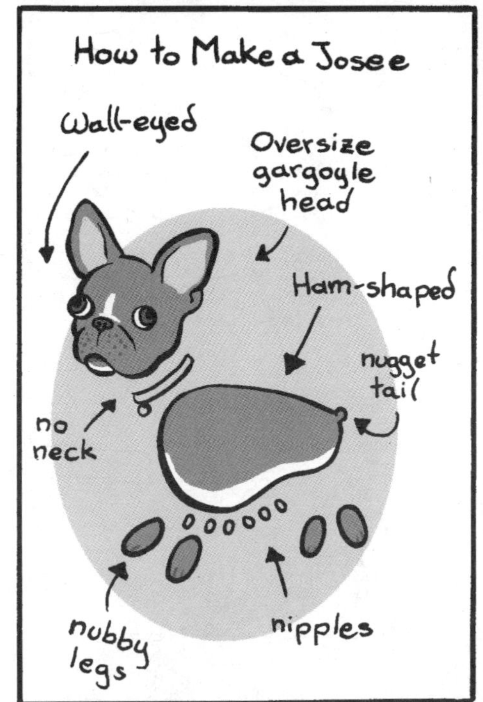
How to Make a Josee
Wall-eyed
Oversize gargoyle head
Ham-shaped
nugget tail
no neck
nubby legs
nipples

No matter how cute it is,
groonk shruf shnrlfle snurk
DON'T PLAY WITH HER TAIL

Dude, you totally gave Josee anal.
It was an accident!
scrub scrub scrub scrub scrub scrub scrub scrub
BWAH

Perspective

Shaved

Here is the thing:
I've always been a fairly hairy girl.

Until one day I had an impulse...
MROWR

Since then I've tried a variety of styles.
scruff
stripe
naked

PLUSES
Nice'n smooth!
Extra sensitive!
fun to pet!

MINUSES
sss!
Can lead to ingrown hair
and rashy skin.

Now I pretty much stick with an unkempt tuft.
Because it's fun to play with.
twirl
twirl
twirl
The cat is a euphemism

Boogie

snnrrr
shnrf
snrfle
snff
snooorp

pick
pick
dig
scrape
pluck

sniff
sniff
ahhh
wipe

Baby!
I- Is that
a boogie?
I-wah?
No?
YES IT IS!

There's toilet roll
right there!
It was dark!
I was
comfortable!
I didn't want
to wake you up!

Honey,
that's **foul**.
I-
I love you?
Kisses?
Seriously!
you're
FOUL

Life Drawing Jerks

As a life model, I encounter some interesting people...
Do you have plans later?
... from the socially inept...

Would you like some butterscotch?
You ask me this every week.
NO.
...to the somewhat disconcerting

So... do you play?
I- what? What does that even mean?
It's just really important that you remember to **play** before you get married.
... to the straight up creepy.

A FEW GUIDELINES:
① Wait until the model is fully clothed,
You're strikingly beautiful!
before initiating conversation
(uncomfortable)

② Just because you see a model naked,
Do you know who I am?
I was hot shit in the '80s!!
Give me your email.
C'mon, don't waste my time.
does not mean s/he will ever sleep with you.

③ If you must hit on the model,
Wanna grab a drink?
$1 for a three week pose
TIP
at least tip well.

October 15, 2008

Special Wed

I'm fuckin' yer ear!!
WHAG!!
fuck
fuck
fuck

What's WRONG with you, y'harpy???
Pay attention to meeeee

mmyamrr
sKREEEch

CHRIST!
You got spit in my eye!!
You fucked my ear!
slap
slap
slap

Don't touch my glasses!
I'm your wife, I can do whatever I want to you!
You're a bloody witch is what you are!
Douche bag!
Filthy cunt!

We have the Special Ed. of marriages.
We're Special Wed.
fuck
fuck
Pick
pick

Man,
three years ago if someone told me you'd marry a boy and I'd be a lesbian— I would have laughed!
Whoah!
When did you start calling yourself a dyke?

It's just easier to say than "I'm a straight girl whose soulmate is a woman"
Yeah, that's why I've been calling myself "queer"—
it's easier.

I don't really feel like a lesbian, tho'!
It's this whole lifestyle I'm not a part of.
I just love my girl.
The 'lifestyle' is why I have such a hard time letting go.

"Lesbian" is my politics, my social sphere, my aesthetic, it's my IDENTITY.
And then suddenly it got too complicated to call myself that because I love one boy.

Sigh.

Whatever!
We're gettin' laid!

Bug Zapper

ZZZZZZZZZZZZZZZZZZZZZZZZZZZZZZ
ZARP!
tZOT
ZORP
ZAP
ZORT!
FzARP
SHzOT!
tzART!
I like to pretend my IUD works like a bug zapper.
My poor, poor little guys.

The Erika Moen Show

Sometimes I broadcast live as I work on comics.
Welcome back, dudes.

Every Monday at 3:30 Leslie broadcasts as she sculpts her Beastlies.

USTEAM TV
LIVE
ON AIR
MENU

You watch these lumps of clay take shape and it's **FASCINATING.**

My cam isn't strong enough to focus on my artwork,
Uh, ohm...
I'm, oh, sketching?
so I just point it at my face like a cam whore.

EoooOooOoo
musn't... be ...boring!
ZWOOP
ZWOOP
ZWOOP
What should take 2 hours turns into 5 or more.

Don't get me wrong, I do love talking with my readers, but...
I'm sweaty, I drew like crap, I acted like an asshole...
Man, I should never do this again.

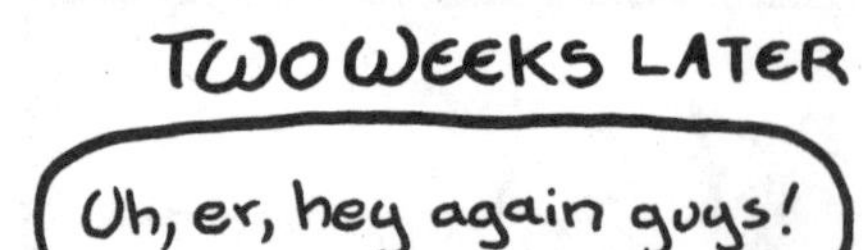
TWO WEEKS LATER
Oh, er, hey again guys!

Who're you talking to?
USTEAM TV
ON AIR
MENU

What can I say?
I like attention.

Gecko

NIP!
yowch!
HEY!
If I bite off your nipple, will it grow back like a gecko's?
No!
BOO!
What are you doing??
Just seeing if you drop a nip when you're startled.
I'm not a gecko!
ZOP!
a-HAH!

Making Home

My home décor is a cross between 'dorm' and 'squatter'
Posters tacked up
novelty lights
desk
work tables
cardboard boxes
tired old beanbags
permanently stained carpet
Bikes against wall

We need a couch.
Don't those cost money?
Plastic plates
Watching Heroes
Alas, I am a bachelorette no longer.

I'm scaaaared.

I guess things do look better off the floor.

One nightstand, throwrug, a set of ceramic dishes, two bookcases, 20 picture frames and several hours of assembly later...

...wow...
It's starting to feel like home.

The Cocktail Party

Russian Brewlette

Have too much tea?
Make a
RUSSIAN ROULETTE
TEA JAR

THE RULES
① Put all your tea in a jar
② You must drink your pick
③ NO PEEKING
Whimper!

slllp
Ceylon Orange Pekoe

Tastes like... dirt?
Some herbal crap

Sploo! Splut!
Eggptian Licorice Mint (the WORST)

ahhh...
Earl Gray
(Make sure you throw a few good ones in too.)

TIPS for CONTROLLING COMPULSIVE BEHAVIOR
I've been struggling with Compulsive Skin Picking since adolescence.

IDENTIFY TRIGGERS
J-just this one...
Mirrors are where I lose self control.

AIR URGES
Baby? I wanna pick.
Too bad.

FIND an ALTERNATIVE PRESSURE RELEASE
5
6
7
8
'Girl' pushups, cos I'm weak

BE ACCOUNTABLE
I'ma pee.
I won't pick.
Good!

BLOCKADE TEMPTATION
I'd never made it two weeks before.
DON'T PICK
The urge is just as strong as its ever been.

One Year

JANUARY
Good news!
We'll save so much money by reducing your hours!
Actually...
You're kinda useless.
But I haven't fired you out of the kindness of my heart.
Work Became Miserable

FEBRUARY
Too Depressed to Move

MARCH
It's time to get back on anti-depressants.
Rx
Returned to Therapy

APRIL
HLUUURG
Adjusted to Medication
Tea?
Repaired Broken Bridges

MAY
20 Minutes After My Job Folded,
Portland, OR
Kent, England
I bought tickets to visit Matt for a Month.

JUNE
It's... almost enough to live on.
Guv'mint
Got on Unemployment

One Year

JULY
Things Are Still Hard...
AUGUST
Life modeling
Picking up odd jobs
Depression and anxiety improving
Periscope Studio
Socializing again
...But Getting Better.

SEPTEMBER
Matt Came to visit Portland

OCTOBER
Signed my First Book Contract
I do
Spontaneous Marriage

NOVEMBER
YES WE CAN

DECEMBER
I've... I've never been so happy.

THE END
Wait!
Wait!
This isn't quite over yet!

For one, there's still some extra stuff here just for this book...

...and for two, you can read even more DAR on it's website at...

www. darcomic. com
fart!

Backgrounds

Because I hate drawing backgrounds, I typically do them once and then just drop them into the comic through the magic of Photoshop.

How many times can you spot each of these throughout the book?

Activity Page

Are you totally diggin' on my art? Learn how to do it yourself!

Okay, so observe a real(istic) person. We'll use Venus by Bouguereau for reference.

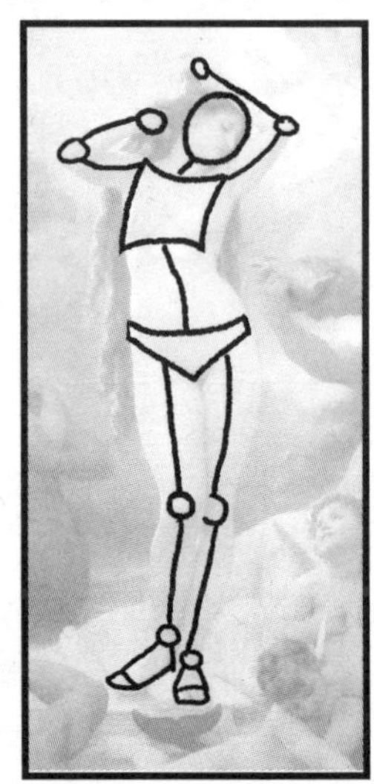

Break her down to her simplest structural skeleton.

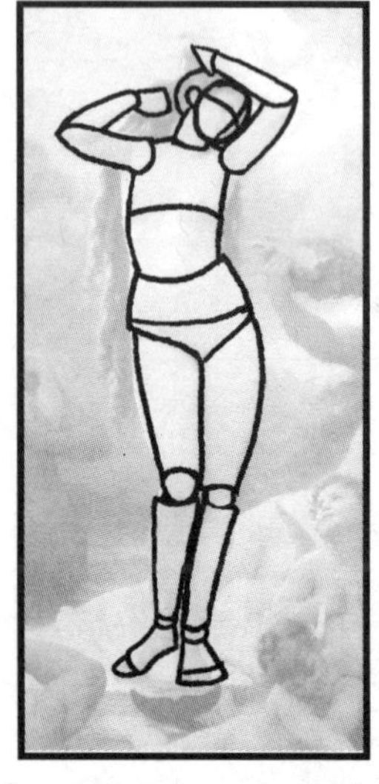

DAR is all about tubes n' round shapes, so draw those over the skeleton.

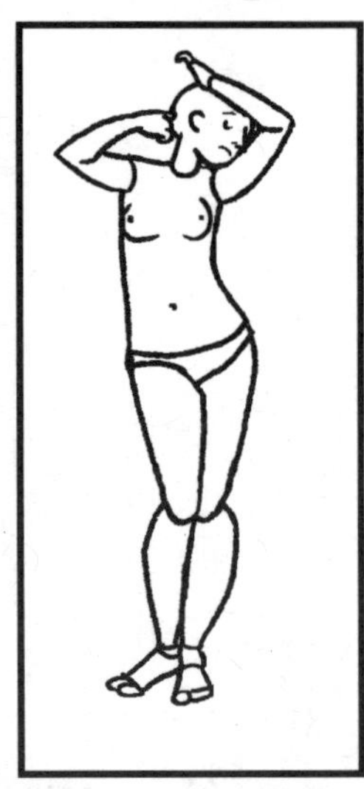

Flesh out those tubes to give them a human touch. Deviate and exaggerate.

Inking adds depth and gives your lines an organic feel. (I use a brush)

Throw on a strap-on and you're drawin' like me! Now go have fun!

About the Cover

Believe it or not, every single person on the cover exists in REAL LIFE!

Thank you so much to my friends for letting me use their (or their dogs') pretty faces.

1. C. Spike Trotman (ironspike.com)
2. Leslie Levings (beastlies.com)
3. Indigo Kelleigh (lunarbistrocom)
4. Josee Lane (twitter.com/joseelane)
5. Bill Mudron (excelsiorstudios.net)
6. Kip Manley (longstoryshortpier.com)
7. Adam Dixon (twitter.com/atomicant)
8. Douglas Wolk (lacunae.com)
9. Matthew Nolan (internationalhobo.com)
10. Dylan Meconis (dylanmeconis.com)
11. Lucy Knisley (lucyknisley.com)
12. Sarah frazier (twitter.com/schmelectra)
13. Brenna Zedan (bzedan.com)
14. R. Stevens (dieselsweeties.com)
15. Jenn Manley Lee (dicebox.net)
16. Steve Lieber (stevelieber.com)
17. Christina Crow (twitter.com/lovemotionstory)
18. Lori Matsumoto (twitter.com/looori)
19. Kaebel Hashitani (sequentialartgallery.com

Interested in visiting some of the places I've mentioned? I don't blame you, they're pretty bitchin'!

Stumptown Comics Fest
stumptowncomics.com
Portland, Oregon
(Pages 41-42, 66)

BunnyLuv
Rabbit Resource Center
bunnyluv.org
(Page 9)

Dr. Sketchy's
Anti-Art School
drsketchy.com
(Page 53)

Devil's Point
devilspointbar.com
5305 SE Foster Road
Portland, OR 97206
(Pages 24, 43)

Acropolis Steakhouse
myspace.com/theacropolissteakhouse
8325 SE Mcloughlin Blvd
Portland, OR 97202
(Page 79)

Blend
Coffee House and Cafe
2327 E Burnside St
Portland, OR 97214
(Page 27)

Knole Park
Sevenoaks,
Kent TN15 0RP
England
(Page 44)

About the Pervert

By Lucy Knisley

Erika Moen was born June 25, 1983 in Seattle, Washington. In 2006 she graduated from Pitzer College with a self-designed degree in Illustrated Storytelling and moved to Portland, Oregon. She is currently a freelance cartoonist and is wondering how long she can keep that up before she has to get a Real Job again. Her sexy British husband, Matthew Nolan, does his best to remind her to eat three times a day and to put on clean clothes every now and then.

www.erikamoen.com

Thank You

Jeff Zugale, Rachel Edindin and Jenn Manley Lee for helping assemble this book.

Dylan Meconis, Leslie Levings, Persicope Studio as a whole and specially Steve Lieber, fabienne and my British family, Anne Moloney and foley, Kip and Taran Jack Manley, Katie Lane, Matt Bernier, Lucy Knisley, Hope Larson, Katie Moody, Jacq Cohen, Kaebel Hashitani, Bill Mudron, Indigo Kelleigh, Scott McCloud, Stumptown Comics fest, Joey Manley, Pitzer College and Al Wachtel, David Kelly and Lin Lucas at The Northwest School, Anita Katz, Derek Kirk Kim, Meredith Gran, Rich Stevens, Danielle Corsetto, Webcomics Weekly, Raymonde Lagune, Stormy and Rocket at Devil's Point, SGPDX, my family and, at the risk of sounding totally corny, everyone who as been following my comics online and encouraging me over the last decade.

And most especially to
Matthew Nolan,
for being my best friend, constant support and editor.
Oh, and for the sex.

This book collects DAR: A Super Girly Top Secret Comic Diary from 2006-2009.

Published by
Erika Moen
4110 SE Hawthorne #225
Portland, OR 97214
www.darcomic.com
www.erikamoen.com

First Edition April 2009

ISBN: 978-0-9823437-0-8

10 8 6 4 2 1 3 5 7 9

Printed in Canada

for questions, complaints, and orders, email erika.moen@gmail.com.